Thanksgivi...

Create a pattern to ...

Copyright © 2022

DEDICATION

Contents

Thanksgiving Turkey Crochet

Here's what you will need:

- worsted weight yarn in brown, yellow, tan, and orange or 4 coordinating colors of your choice

- a small amount of red, white, and black worsted weight yarn for the face

- US G-6 / 4.0mm crochet hook

- fiberfill stuffing or yarn scraps

- stitch marker, tapestry needle, and scissors

Thanksgiving Crochet

Resources and tutorials you may find helpful in following this crochet pattern: Crochet Abbreviations, U.S. to U.K. Crochet Conversion Chart, How to Make a Magic Ring {photo & video tutorial}.

Add this pattern to your Ravelry library.

BODY

Body is worked in unjoined rounds. You may find it helpful to use a stitch marker to keep track of rounds.

With brown, make a magic ring (as an alternative to the magic ring, you can ch 4 and join with a slip stitch in furthest chain from hook to form a ring).

Round 1: Ch 1 (does not count as st), work 6 sc in ring — 6 sts.

Round 2: Work 2 sc in each st around — 12 sts.

Round 3: *Work 2 sc in next st, 1 sc in next st, rep from * around — 18 sts.

Round 4: *Work 2 sc in next st, 1 sc in each of the next 2 sts, rep from * around — 24 sts.

Rounds 5 through 8: Work 1 sc in each st around — 24 sts.

Thanksgiving Crochet

Round 9: *Sc2tog, 1 sc in each of the next 2 sts, rep from * around — 18 sts.

Rounds 10 through 12: Work 1 sc in each st around — 18 sts.

Round 13: *Work 2 sc in next st, 1 sc in each of the next 2 sts, rep from * around — 24 sts.

Round 14: *Work 2 sc in next st, 1 sc in each of the next 3 sts, rep from * around — 30 sts.

Round 15: *Work 2 sc in next st, 1 sc in each of the next 4 sts, rep from * around — 36 sts.

Rounds 16 through 21: Work 1 sc in each st around — 36 sts.

Round 22: *Sc2tog, 1 sc in each of the next 4 sts, rep from * around — 30 sts.

Round 23: *Sc2tog, 1 sc in each of the next 3 sts, rep from * around — 24 sts.

Round 24: *Sc2tog, 1 sc in each of the next 2 sts, rep from * around — 18 sts.

Round 25: *Sc2tog, 1 sc in next st, rep from * around — 12 sts.

Fill body with fiberfill stuffing or yarn scraps taking care not to overstuff.

Round 26: Sc2tog around — 6 sts.

Fasten off leaving approximately a 6-in. tail. Using a tapestry needle and the tail, weave opening closed.

BEAK

With yellow, ch 4.

Row 1: Work 1 sc in 2nd ch from hook and each ch across, turn — 3 sts.

Row 2: Ch 1 (does not count as st), skip 1st st, sc2tog — 1 st.

Fasten off leaving a long enough tail to sew beak to the face.

EYES

With white, ch 7.

Row 1: Work 2 dc in 4th ch from hook, ch 1, work 1 sc in next st, ch1, work 2 dc in next st, ch 2, Sl st in next.

Fasten off leaving a long enough tail to sew eyes to the face. Using a tapestry needle and black yarn, make a french knot in the center of each eye for pupils.

SNOOD

(or "the red thingy" as I was calling it until I Googled it)

With red, ch 8.

Row 1: Work 3 sc in 2nd ch from hook and each ch across — 21 sts.

Fasten off leaving a long enough tail to sew the red thingy to the face.

FINISHING THE FACE

Using a tapestry needle and long tails left, sew the eyes, beak, and snood to the turkey's head as shown below …

Thanksgiving Crochet

WINGS

Make 5 granny squares in all. Make 3 squares following the color sequence below; make 2 squares using CC for Round 1 and CA for Round 3. These granny squares are also a great opportunity to practice those standing stitches I showed you how to do in my post here.

CA = yellow; CB = tan; CC = orange; CD = brown

With CA, make a magic ring.

Round 1: Ch 3 (counts as st), work 2 dc in ring, ch 3, *3 dc in ring, ch 3, repeat from *twice more, join in top of beg ch, fasten off — 12 sts.

Round 2: Join CB in any ch-3 sp, ch 3 (counts as st), 2 dc in same ch-3 sp, ch 2, *[3 dc, ch 3, 3 dc] in next ch-3 sp, ch 2, rep from * twice more, 3 dc in same ch-3 sp as first st of round, ch 3, join in top of beg ch, fasten off — 24 sts.

Round 3: Join CC in any ch-3 corner sp, ch 3 (counts as st), 2 dc in same ch-3 sp, *ch 2, 3 dc in next ch-2 sp, ch 2, [3 dc, ch 3, 3 dc] in next ch-3 corner sp, rep from * twice more, ch 2, 3 dc in next ch-2 sp, ch 2, 3 dc in same ch-3 corner sp as first st of round, ch 3, join in top of beg ch, fasten off — 36 sts.

Round 4: Join CD in any ch-3 corner sp, work 3 sc in same ch-3 sp, *work 1 sc in each of the next 3 sts, work 2 sc in next ch-2 sp, work 1 sc in each of the next 3 sts, work 2 sc in next ch-2 sp, work 1 sc in each of the next 3 sts, work 3 sc in ch-3 corner sp, rep from * twice more, work 1 sc in each of the next 3 sts, work 2 sc in next ch-2 sp, work 1 sc in each of the next 3 sts, work 2 sc in next ch-2 sp, work 1 sc in each of the next 3 sts, join, fasten off — 64 sts.

FINISHING

Take 2 of the 3 A-B-C-D color sequence granny squares and slip stitch or sew together on one edge as shown below.

Take the 2 C-B-A-D color sequence grannies and lay them on top as shown below. Sew a stitch or two to each to secure in place.

Take the last A-B-C-D color sequence granny square and lay on top as shown below. Sew a stitch or two to secure in place.

Lay the turkey body on the granny squares.

Roll the bottom squares around the bottom of the turkey body and stitch into place. Check the wings and stitch where necessary to make secure.

Tasty Turkey Basket

Add this pattern to your Ravelry Queue and Favorites

- US – I, 5.5mm hook (Furls Fiberarts recommended)

- US – K, 6.5mm hook (Clover Amour Jumbo Hook recommended)

- 625 yds Bulky yarn (original yarn is discontinued)
  Color A: Coffee – 450 yds

Thanksgiving Crochet

Color B: Pumpkin – 65 yds

Color C: Black – 10 yds

Color D: Honey – 65 yds

Color E: Cranberry – 5 yds

Color F: Avocado – 30 yds

- Gauge: 10 sts x 8 rows = 4" in hdc with yarn held doubled and larger hook

- Finished Size: Basket portion = 10" long x 6" wide x 5" high

- Helpful video tutorials: Bag Bottoms (rows to rounds); Hdc Decreases; Magic Circle

NOTE: Some parts are made with the yarn held doubled and the larger hook, others are made with the yarn held singly and the smaller hook – this is listed at the beginning of that part of the pattern.

BASKET INSTRUCTIONS: Make 1, with Color A, yarn held doubled, larger hook

Row 1: Ch 24, skip the ch closest to the hook, hdc in each of the remaining chs; turn. (23 sts)

Row 2 – 12: Ch 1, hdc 23; turn. (23 sts)

Round 13: Ch 1, hdc 23, turn work 90°, hdc 14 along sides of previous rows, turn work 90°, hdc 23 along foundation chain, turn work 90°, hdc 14 along sides of previous rows; join to first hdc of round with a sl st. (74 sts)

Round 14 – 22: Ch 1, hdc in each st around; join with a sl st. (74 sts) After Round 22, break yarn and finish off.

HEAD INSTRUCTIONS: Make 1, with Color A, yarn held doubled, larger hook

Row 1: Ch 10, skip the ch closest to the hook, hdc in each of the remaining chs; turn. (9 sts)

Row 2 – 4: Ch 1, hdc 9; turn. (9 sts)

Row 5: Ch 1, hdc2tog, hdc 5, hdc2tog; turn. (7 sts)

Row 6 – 7: Ch 2, hdc 7; turn. (7 sts)

Row 8: Ch 1, hdc2tog, hdc 3, hdc2tog; turn. (5 sts)

Row 9 – 10: Ch 1, hdc 5; turn. (5 sts)

Row 11: Ch 1, 2 hdc in the 1st st, hdc 3, 2 hdc in the last st; turn. (7 sts)

Row 12 – 13: Ch 1, hdc 7; turn. (7 sts)

Row 14: Ch 1, hdc2tog, hdc 3, hdc2tog; turn. (5 sts)

Row 15: Ch 1, hdc2tog, hdc, hdc2tog; turn. (3 sts)

Edge: Ch 1, sc evenly all around head; break yarn leaving a long tail for sewing.

BEAK INSTRUCTIONS: Make 1, with Color B, yarn held singly, smaller hook

Row 1: Ch 6, skip the ch closest to the hook, sc in each remaining ch; turn. (5 sts)

Row 2: Ch 1, sc2tog, sc in the next st, sc2tog; turn. (3 sts)

Row 3: Ch 1, sc3tog; break yarn leaving long tail for sewing. (1 st)

Sew beak to head as shown.

EYES INSTRUCTIONS: Make 2, with Color C, yarn held singly, smaller hook

Round 1: Starting with a magic circle, hdc 10 in the ring; join with a sl st and break yarn, leaving long tail for sewing. (10 sts)

Add "twinkle" with yarn needle and a small amount of Color D.

Sew eyes to head as shown.

WATTLE INSTRUCTIONS: Make 1, with Color E, yarn held single, smaller hook

Row 1: Ch 9, skip the 2 chs closest to the hook, dc in next 3 chs, hdc in next 2 chs, sc in next ch, sl st in last ch; break yarn and finish off, leaving a long tail for sewing.

Sew wattle to head as shown.

TAIL FEATHER INSTRUCTIONS: All made with yarn held doubled, larger hook

- Make 1 with Color F

- Make 2 with Color B

- Make 2 with Color D

Row 1: Ch 2, skip the ch closest to the hook, 3 dc in last ch; turn. (3 sts)

Row 2: Ch 2, 2 dc in the 1st st, dc in the next st, 2 dc in the last st; turn. (5 sts)

Row 3 – 7: Ch 2, dc in each st across; turn. (5 sts)

Row 8: Ch 2, dc2tog, dc in next st, dc2tog; turn. (3 sts)

Row 9: Ch 2, dc3tog; turn. (1 st)

Edge: Ch 1, sc evenly all around feather; break yarn leaving a long tail to sew it to the basket with.

ASSEMBLY: After sewing the beak, eyes, and wattle to the head, sew the head and tail feathers to the baske

Fabulous Fall Table Runner

Crochet HookH/8 or 5 mm hook

Yarn Weight (4) Medium Weight/Worsted Weight and Aran (16-20 stitches to 4 inches)

Crochet Gauge14 dc = 4 (10 cm); 8 rows = 4 (10 cm). CHECK YOUR GAUGE. Use any size hook to obtain the gauge.

Thanksgiving Crochet

Materials

RED HEART® With Love®: 1 skein each 1

401 Pewter A

1201 Daffodil B

1909 Holly Berry C

1252 Mango D

1530 Violet E

Note: Only small quantities of B, C, D, and E are needed for this project.

Susan Bates® Crochet Hook: 5mm [US H-8]

Yarn needle

Runner measures 14" wide x 39" long (35.5 x 99 cm), excluding leaves.

Notes

Runner is worked from center out to curved ends. Leaves are made separately and sewn to runner.

Thanksgiving Crochet

Runner

First side

With A, ch 51.

Row 1 (right side): Dc in 4th ch from hook (beginning ch count as first dc) and in each ch across, turn—49 dc.

Row 2: Ch 1, sc in first dc, *ch 2, skip next 2 dc, dc in next dc, ch 2, skip next 2 dc, sc in next dc; repeat from * across ending with

last sc in 3rd ch of beginning ch, turn—9 sc, 8 dc, and 16 ch-2 spaces.

Row 3: Ch 3 (counts as first dc here and throughout), 2 dc in first sc, sc in next dc, *5 dc in next sc, sc in next dc; repeat from * to

last sc, 3 dc in last sc, turn—8 sc and 41 dc.

Row 4: Repeat Row 2.

Row 5: Ch 3, 2 dc in first ch-2 space, dc in next dc, 2 dc in next ch-2 space, dc in next sc, *2 dc in next ch-2 space, dc in next dc, 2

dc in next ch-2 space, dc in next sc; repeat from * across, turn—49 dc.

Row 6: Repeat Row 2.

Thanksgiving Crochet

Rows 7–30: Repeat Rows 3–6 six times.

Rows 31 and 32: Repeat Rows 3 and 4.

Row 33: Ch 1, slip st in first sc, slip st in first ch-2 space, slip st in next dc, slip st in next ch-2 space, slip st in next sc, ch 3, *2 dc in next ch-2 space, dc in next dc, 2 dc in next ch-2 space, dc in next sc; repeat from * 5 times; leave remaining sts and spaces unworked, turn—37 dc.

Row 34: Repeat Row 6.

Rows 35 and 36: Repeat Rows 3 and 4—7 sc, 6 dc, and 12 ch-2 spaces.

Row 37: Ch 1, slip st in first sc, slip st in first ch-2 space, slip st in next dc, slip st in next ch-2 space, slip st in next sc, ch 3, *2 dc in next ch-2 space, dc in next dc, 2 dc in next ch-2 space, dc in next sc; repeat from * 4 times; leave remaining sts and spaces unworked, turn—25 dc.

Row 38 and 39: Repeat Rows 2 and 3—6 sc and 26 dc.

Fasten off.

2nd Side

Row 1 (right side): With right side facing and working in opposite side of foundation ch, join A with slip st in first ch, ch 3, dc in each ch across, turn—49 dc.

Rows 2–39: Repeat Rows 2–39 of first side.

Walk This Way Turkey Pattern

Crochet HookF/5 or 3.75 mm hook

Yarn Weight (4) Medium Weight/Worsted Weight and Aran (16-20 stitches to 4 inches)

MATERIALS:

RED HEART® Super Saver®: 1 skein each

A: 360 Cafe Latte

B: 321 Gold

C: 256 Carrot

D: 319 Cherry Red

E: 312 Black

Susan Bates® Crochet Hook: (F/5 or 3.75 mm)

Yarn needle

Fiberfill

SIZE:

Turkey measures 7" (18 cm).

GAUGE:

Gauge is not critical for this project.

SPECIAL STITCHES:

sc2tog = [Insert hook in next stitch, yarn over and draw up a loop] twice, yarn over and draw through all 3 loops on hook.

sc3tog = [Insert hook in next stitch, yarn over and draw up a loop] 3 times, yarn over and draw through all 4 loops on hook.

TURKEY

Thanksgiving Crochet

HEAD AND BODY

Note: Stuff piece as work progresses for best results.

Beginning at top of head with A, ch 2.

Round 1: Work 6 sc in second ch from hook; join with slip st in first sc – 6 sc.

Round 2: Ch 1, 2 sc in each st around; join with slip st in first st – 12 sc.

Round 3: Ch 1, [sc in next st, 2 sc in next st] 6 times; join with slip st in first st – 18 sc.

Round 4: Ch 1, [sc in each of next 2 sts, 2 sc in next st] 6 times; join with slip st in first st – 24 sc.

Rounds 5-8: Ch1, sc in each st around; join with slip st in first st.

Round 9: Ch 1, [sc in next 2 sts, sc2tog] 6 times; join with slip st in first st – 18 sc.

Round 10: Ch 1, [sc in next st, sc2tog] 6 times; join with slip st in first st – 12 sc.

Round 11: Ch 1, sc2tog around; join with slip st in first st – 6 sc.

Round 12: Ch1, [2 sc in next st] 6 times; join with slip st in first st – 12 sc.

Round 13: Ch 1, [sc in next st, 2 sc in next st] 6 times; join with slip st in first st – 18 sc.

Round 14: Ch 1, [sc in next 2 sts, 2 sc in next st] 6 times; join with slip st in first st – 24 sc.

Round 15: Ch 1, [sc in next 3 sts, 2 sc in next st] 6 times; join with slip st in first st – 30 sc.

Rounds 16-20: Ch 1, sc in each st around; join with slip st in first st.

Round 21: Ch 1, [sc in next 3 sts, sc2tog] 6 times; join with slip st in first st – 24 sc.

Round 22: Ch 1, [sc in next 2 sts, sc2tog] 6 times; join with slip st in first st – 18 sc.

Round 23: Ch 1, [sc in next st, sc2tog] 6 times; join with slip st in first st – 12 sc.

Round 24: Ch 1, sc2tog around; join with slip st in first st – 6 sc. Fasten off.

TAIL FEATHERS

With A, ch 2.

Round 1: Work 6 sc in second ch from hook; join with slip st in first st – 6 sc.

Round 2: Ch 1, [2 sc in next st] 6 times; join with slip st in first st – 12 sc.

Round 3: Ch 1, [sc in next st, 2 sc in next st] 6 times; join with slip st in first st – 18 sc.

Round 4: Ch 1, [sc in next 2 sts, 2 sc in next st] 6 times; join with slip st in first st – 24 sc.

Round 5: Ch 1, [sc in next 3 sts, 2 sc in next st] 6 times; join with slip st in first st – 30 sc.

Note: Work progresses in rows from this point.

Row 6: Fold piece in half; working through

both thicknesses, sc in next st, [ch 5, sc in next st] 14 times – 14 ch-5 spaces. Fasten off A.

Row 7: Join B with sc in first ch-5 space of Row 6, [ch 5, sc in next st] 13 times – 13 ch-5 spaces. Fasten off B.

Row 8: Join D with sc in first ch-5 space of Row 7, [ch 5, sc in next st] 12 times – 12 ch-5 spaces. Fasten off D.

Row 8: Join C with sc in first ch-5 space of Row 8, [ch 5, sc in next st] 11 times – 11 ch-5 spaces. Fasten off C.

BEAK

With B, ch 2.

Round 1: Work 6 sc in second ch from hook; join with slip st in first st – 6 sc.

Round 2-3: Ch 1, sc in each st around; join with slip st in first st.

Round 4: Ch 1, sc in next 3 sts, leave remaining sts unworked – 3 sc. Fasten off leaving long tail for sewing. Stuff lightly.

SNOOD

Thanksgiving Crochet

With D, ch 5.

Row 1: Sc in second ch from hook, sc in next 3 chs; turn – 4 sc.

Row 2-3: Ch1, sc in each st across; turn.

Row 4: Ch 1, [sc2tog] twice; turn – 2 sc.

Row 5-6: Ch 1, sc in each st across; turn.

Row 7: Ch 1, sc2tog – 1 sc. Fasten off, leaving long tail for sewing.

ARMS (Make 2)

With A, ch 8; join with slip st to form a ring.

Round 1: Ch 1, sc in each ch around; join with slip st in first st – 8 sc.

Rounds 2-7: Ch 1, sc in each st around; join with slip st in first st.

Note: Stuff arm. Work progresses in rows from this point.

Row 8: Fold piece in half; ch 1, working through both thicknesses, sc in each st across to close; turn – 4 sc.

Row 9: [ch 3, slip st in second ch from hook, slip st in next ch, slip st in next sc] 4 times – 4 fingers. Fasten off.

FEET (Make 2)

Round 1: With B, ch 5, 3 sc in second ch from hook, sc in next ch, 3 sc in next sc, sc in last ch; join with slip st in first st – 8 sc.

Round 2: Ch 1, [2 sc in next 3 sts, sc in next st] twice; join with slip st in first st – 14 sc.

Round 3: Ch 1, sc in each st around; join with slip st in first st.

Round 4: Ch 1, sc in next 9 sts, sc3tog, sc in next 2 sts; join with slip st in first st – 12 sc.

Round 5: Ch 1, sc in next 8 sts, sc3tog, sc in next st; join with slip st in first st – 10 sc.

Round 6-9: Ch 1, sc in each st around; join with slip st in first st. Fasten off, leaving long tail for sewing. Stuff Leg.

FINISHING

Using photo as a guide, sew Beak to middle front of Head. Sew the snood to side of Beak. Sew Tail Feather piece to back side of Body. Sew Arms three rows down from neck. Sew Legs to bottom of Body. With E, whipstitch eyes. Weave in all ends.

Crochet **Turkey Amigurumi**

MATERIALS

Crochet Hook: 3.0mm & 4.5mm

DK Acrylic yarn in Dark Brown, Yellow, Brown, White and Red colors

Polyester fiberfill

Thanksgiving Crochet

12mm Black Safety Eye, 1 pair

TOOLS

Darning needle (Long)

Fabric marker (water erasable)

Scissors

Pins

A pair of blunt point tweezers for stuffing small parts

INSTRUCTIONS

Crochet and stuff all parts by following the crochet patterns stated below to make Body, Head, Eye-White, Beak, Snood, Wing, Feet and lastly, the beautiful Tail.

Assemble the head with eyes, beak, and snood.

Sew body to the head followed by wings, feet, and tail to the body

Add some strips of short yarns onto the top of the head.

ABBREVIATIONS (US TERMS)

Thanksgiving Crochet

ch: chain

BS : *Bubble Stitch

dc: double crochet

hdc: half double crochet

sc: single crochet

inc: 2sc increase

inv dec: invisible decrease

ps3: puff stitch (hdc3tog)

*Bubble Stitch: Yarn over (YO), hook through ch and pull up a loop, YO and pull through 2 loops on hook. Repeat the same step in the same ch till you get 5 loops on hook, YO and pull through all 5 loops on hook.

TURKEY AMIGURUMI CROCHET PATTERN

BODY

With Dark Brown yarn and 3mm hook:

Round 1: ch5, Inc in 2nd ch from hook, sc 2, 5sc in the last ch.

Thanksgiving Crochet

Continue on the other side of the chain base, sc 2, 3sc in the last ch. {14}

Round 2: Inc, sc 4, [Inc] 3 times, sc 4, [Inc] 2 times. {20}

Round 3: Inc, sc 6, [Inc] 2 times, sc, Inc, sc 6, [Inc] 2 times, sc. {26}

Round 4: Inc, sc 8, [Inc, sc] 2 times, Inc, sc 8, [Inc, sc] 2 times. {32}

Round 5: Inc, sc 10, Inc, sc 2, Inc, sc, Inc, sc 10, Inc, sc 2, Inc, sc. {38}

Round 6: Inc. sc 12, [Inc, sc 2] 2 times, Inc, sc 12, [Inc, sc 2] 2 times. {44}

Round 7: Inc, sc 14, Inc, sc 3, Inc, sc 2, Inc, sc 14, Inc, sc 3, Inc, sc 2. {50}

Round 8: Inc, sc 16, [Inc, sc 3] 2 times, Inc, sc 16, [Inc, sc 3] 2 times. {56}

Round 9: sc around. {56}

Round 10: sc 25, Inc, sc 27, Inc, sc 2. {58}

Round 11: sc 26, Inc, sc 28, Inc, sc 2. {60}

Round 12: sc 27, Inc, sc 29, Inc, sc 2. {62}

Round 13: sc 28, Inc, sc 30, Inc, sc 2. {64}

Round 14 – 21: sc around. {64}

Round 22: sc 6, [Inv dec, sc 14] 3 times, Inv dec, sc 8. {60}

Round 23: sc around. {60}

Round 24: sc 6, [Inv dec, sc 13] 3 times, Inv dec, sc 7. {56}

Round 25: sc around. {56}

Round 26: sc 6, [Inv dec, sc 12] 3 times, Inv dec, sc 6. {52}

Round 27: [Inv dec, sc 11] 4 times. {48}

Round 28: sc 6, [Inv dec, sc 10] 3 times, Inv dec, sc 4. {44}

Round 29: [Inv dec, sc 9] 4 times. {40}

Round 30: sc 6, [Inv dec, sc 8] 3 times, Inv dec, sc 2. {36}

Round 31: [Inv dec, sc 7] 4 times. {32}

Round 32: [sc 6, Inv dec] 4 times. {28}

Round 33: sc around. {28}

Round 34: [sc 5, Inv dec] 4 times. {24}

Round 35: sc around. {24}

Stuff the body firmly with polyester fiberfill.

Round 36: [sc 4, Inv dec] 4 times. {20}

Round 37: sc around. {20}

Round 38: [sc 3, Inv dec] 4 times. {16}

Round 39 - 43 : sc around. {16}

Round 44: [Inv dec] 8 times. {8}

Fasten and hide yarn end.

HEAD

With Dark Brown yarn and 3mm hook:

Round 1: sc 6 in magic ring. {6}

Round 2: [inc] 6 times. {12}

Round 3: [sc, inc] 6 times. {18}

Round 4: sc around. {18}

Round 5: [inc, sc 2] 6 times. {24}

Thanksgiving Crochet

Round 6: sc around. {24}

Round 7: [sc3, inc] 6 times. {30}

Round 8: sc around. {30}

Round 9: sc 2, [inc, sc 4] 5 times, inc, sc 2. {36}

Round 10: sc around. {36}

Round 11: [sc5, inc] 6 times. {42}

Round 12: sc around. {42}

Round 13: sc 3, [inc, sc 6] 5 times, inc, sc 3. {48}

Round 14: sc around. {48}

Round 15: [sc 7, inc] 6 times. {54}

Round 16: sc around. {54}

Round 17: sc 4, [inc, sc 8] 5 times, inc, sc 4. {60}

Round 18 - 24: sc around. {60}

Install eyes at round 16. Hide white yarn end into the head.

Round 25: sc 4, [inv dec, sc 8] 5 times, inv dec, sc 4. {54}

Round 26: [inv dec, sc 7] 6 times. {48}

Round 27: sc 3, [inv dec, sc 6] 5 times, inv dec, sc 3. {42}

Round 28: [inv dec, sc 5] 6 times. {36}

Round 29: sc 2, [inv dec, sc 4] 5 times, inv dec, sc 2. {30}

Round 30: [inv dec, sc 3] 6 times. {24}

Stuff with polyester fillings.

Round 31: sc, [inv dec, sc 2] 5 times, inv dec, sc. {18}

Round 32: [inv dec, sc] 6 times. {12}

Round 33: [inv dec] 6 times. {6}

Fasten and leave a long tail for sewing.

EYE-WHITE

Make 2 with White yarn and 3mm hook:

Round 1: sc 6 in magic ring. {6}

Round 2: [inc] around. {12}

Round 3: [inc, sc] around. {18}

Fasten and leave a long tail for sewing.

Sew 2 circles alongside together (about 2 stitches) to form the eye-white.

BEAK

With Yellow yarn and 3mm hook:

Round 1: Sc 4 in magic ring. {4}

Round 2: sc around. {4}

Round 3: [inc, sc] 2 times. {6}

Round 4: sc around. {6}

Fasten and leave a long tail for sewing.

SNOOD

With Red yarn and 3mm hook:

Round 1: Sc 4 in magic ring. {4}

Round 2: [inc] around. {8}

Round 3: [sc 3, inc] 2 times. {10}

Round 4 - 6: sc around. {10}

Round 7: [inv dec, sc 3] 2 times. {8}

Round 8: sc around. {8}

Stuff with polyester fillings or red yarn scraps.

Round 9: sc, [inv dec, sc 2], inv dec, sc. {6}

Round 10: sc around. {6}

Round 11: [inv dec, sc] 2 times. {4}

Round 12 - 26: sc around. {4}

Fasten and leave a long tail for sewing.

WINGS

Make 2 starting with Brown yarn and 3mm hook:

Round 1: sc 6 in magic ring. {6}

Round 2: [inc] 6 times. {12}

Round 3: [inc, sc] 6 times. {18}

Round 4: [sc 2, inc] 6 times. {24}

Thanksgiving Crochet

Round 5: sc, [inc, sc 3] 5 times, inc, sc 2. {30}

Fold the piece into half and sc across then turn. {15}

Row 6: ch 2, [BS, hdc] 7 times, BS. Turn. {15}

Change yarn to Yellow color

Row 7: ch 1, [sc 2, 2sc in next sc] 5 times. Turn. {20}

Row 8: ch 2, [BS, hdc] 9 times, BS. {20}

Fasten and leave a long tail for sewing.

FEET

Make 2 with Yellow yarn and 3mm hook:

Toe (make 3, name them toe1, toe2, toe3)

Round 1: sc 3 in magic ring. {3}

Round 2: [inc] 3 times. {6}

Round 3 - 6: sc around. {6}

Fasten only 2 toes. Continue to the foot part from 3rd toe.

Foot

Round 7: sc 3 on toe3, sc 3 on toe2, sc around on toe1, sc 3 on toe2, sc 3 on toe3 to join up the toes to the foot. {18}

Round 8: sc around. {18}

Round 9: [inv dec, sc] 6 times. {12}

Round 10: sc around. {12}

Stuff with polyester fillings or yellow yarn scraps.

Round 11: [inv dec] 6 times. {6}

Fasten and leave a long tail for sewing.

TAIL

Make 2 starting with Brown yarn and 4.5mm hook:

Round 1: ch3 (as 1 dc), dc 14 in magic ring. slst to the first st of the round. {15}

Round 2: ch3 (as 1 dc), dc in the same st, [2dc] 14 times. slst to the first st of the round.{30}

Round 3: ch3 (as 1 dc), 2dc, [dc, 2dc] 14 times. slst to the first st of the round. {45}

Thanksgiving Crochet

Change Yarn to Dark Brown color

Round 4: ch 1, sc in same st, sc 44. slst to the first st of the round. {45}
Fasten off but do not cut the yarn of one of the tail. **Reserve the yarn for joining up the tailpieces and outlining (pic Tail 2).

Tail Feather

Change Yarn to White Color

Row 1: (ch3, dc, ch, 2dc) in same st, [skip 2 sts, (2dc, ch, 2dc) in next st] repeat 9 times.

Fasten and hide yarn

Change Yarn to Yellow Color

Row 2: start at the ch space of the previous row, (ch3, dc, ch, 2dc) in the same space, [(2dc, ch, 2dc) in the next ch space] repeat 9 times.

Fasten and hide yarn

Change Yarn to Brown Color

Row 3: start at the ch space of the previous row, (ch3, 2dc, ch, 3dc) in the same space, [(3dc, ch, 3dc) in the next ch space] repeat 9 times.

Fasten and hide yarn

Change Yarn to White Color

Row 4: start at the ch space of the previous row, (ch3, 2dc, ch, 3dc) in the same space, [(3dc, ch, 3dc) in the next ch space] repeat 9 times. fasten and hide yarn

Change Yarn to Brown Color

Row 5 – start at the ch space of the previous row, (ch3, 8dc) in the same space, [9dc in next ch space] repeat 9 times. fasten and hide yarn.

Fasten and hide yarn

TAIL OUTLINE

The tail outlining and detailing are made while joining both layers. All stitches must go through both pieces for joining up.

Place a tailpiece on top of another tailpiece, with the wrong side facing each other. Line up edges.

The bottom arc of the tail: From the yarn reserved** at Round 4, sc across both layers.

Thanksgiving Crochet

The side edge of the tail: *ch 1, sc, repeat * until you reach the corner of the tail. Single crochet 9 stitches on the shell and 1 stitch between the 2 shells

Crochet 1 chain, then single crochet at the space between 2 shells on the following row.

Repeat the stitches until you get to the end of the feather

sc in the first and second skip stitches of round 5.

Crochet 1 chain, then single crochet again between 2 shells on the following row to work up to the top again.

Continue to crochet by repeating the stitches for the rest of the tail details.

Fasten and leave a long tail for sewing. Front. Back

Sew the slanted eyebrows with a short dark brown yarn above the safety eyes. You may create other expressions by altering the angles of the slope.

Parts to be added to the head: head with eyes installed, beak and snood.

Sew the beak below the center of the eye-whites. Followed by sewing the snood enfolded on the top of the beak. Crochet all the parts as per the pattern above and get ready for the final assembly. Sew to join head to the body. Then sew wings followed by the feet to the body. Tutt the turkey amigurumi doesn't feel happy without its beautiful tail attached.

Position the tail on the back of the body, pin.

Sew the bottom arc of the tail to the body.

Sew the rest of the arc of the tail to the body.

The tail is attached but Tutt still feels something missing on its head. Perhaps Tutt wants some hair (or crest) on its head to make it looks better. Cut some shorts strand of yellow yarn and tie them around the tip of the head.

Colorful Crochet Turkey

SUPPLIES

worsted weight yarn in brown, gold, red, green, blue, orange

G crochet hook

6" scrap of fabric

45

2- 9mm black safety eyes

sewing needle

sewing thread

yarn needle

scissors

INSTRUCTIONS

STEP ONE

Begin by making the weighted pouch that will sit inside the base of the turkey.

Cut 6" diameter circle from fabric

Knot one end of the thread and stitch around the outside of the circle with a running stitch

Pull thread to cinch up partway, fill with weighted stuffing beads

Cinch up the rest of the way and stitch through the top a few times to secure

STEP TWO

Crochet the Body

you will begin with a magic ring (mr) and work in the round

with brown yarn

Round 1: in mr, ch 1, 6 sc (6 sc)

Round 2: 2 sc in each stitch (12 sc)

Round 3: [1 sc in first stitch, 2 sc in next], repeat around (18 sc)

Round 4: [1 sc in first 2 stitches, 2 sc in next], repeat around (24 sc)

Round 5: [1 sc in first 3 stitches, 2 sc in next], repeat around (30 sc)

Round 6: [1 sc in first 4 stitches, 2 sc in next], repeat around (36 sc)

Round 7: 1 sc in each stitch (36 sc)

Round 8: [1 sc in first 5 stitches, 2 sc in next], repeat around (42 sc)

Rounds 9-13: 1 sc in each stitch

Round 14: [1 sc in first 5 stitches, sc2tog], repeat around (36 sc)

Round 15: 1 sc in each stitch (36 sc)

Round 16: [1 sc in first 4 stitches, sc2tog], repeat around (30 sc)

Round 17: 1 sc in each stitch (30 sc)

*add weighted pouch to bottom of the body

Round 18: [1 sc in first 3 stitches, sc2tog], repeat around (24 sc)

Round 19: 1 sc in each stitch (24 sc)

*begin stuffing the body and continue stuffing as you work the last couple of rows

Round 20: [1 sc in first 2 stitches, sc2tog], repeat around (18 sc)

Round 21: [1 sc in first stitch, sc2tog], repeat around (12 sc)

Round 22: sc2tog, repeat around (6 sc)

Finish off, tuck yarn end inside of the body

Thanksgiving Crochet

STEP THREE

Crochet the head

begin with a magic ring (mr)

with brown yarn

Round 1: in mr, ch 1, 6 sc (6 sc)

Round 2: 2 sc in each stitch (12 sc)

Round 3: [1 sc in first stitch, 2 sc in next], repeat around (18 sc)

Round 4: [1 sc in first 2 stitches, 2 sc in next], repeat around (24 sc)

Round 5: [1 sc in first 3 stitches, 2 sc in next], repeat around (30 sc)

Rounds 6-10: 1 sc in each stitch (30 sc)

Round 11: [1 sc in first 3 stitches, sc2tog], repeat around (24 sc)

Thanksgiving Crochet

Round 12: [1 sc in first 2 stitches, sc2tog], repeat around (18 sc)

Round 13: 1 sc in each stitch (18 sc)

Finish off, cut yarn leaving long end for sewing

Attach safety eyes, I placed mine between rounds 7 and 8, about 3 stitches apart

Stuff head and sew onto the top of the body (the body is worked from bottom up and the head is worked from top down)

STEP FOUR

Crochet the Wings:

begin with a magic ring (mr)

Make 2- with brown yarn

Row 1: in mr, ch 1, 5 sc (5 sc)

Row 2: ch1, turn, sc, 2 hdc, 2 dc, 2 hdc, sc (2 sc, 4 hdc, 2 dc)

Row 3: ch 1, turn, sc, sc, 2 hdc, 2dc, 2 dc, 2 hdc, sc, sc (4 sc, 4 hdc, 4 dc)

Finish off, cut yarn leaving long end for sewing

Sew wings to the sides of the body

STEP FIVE

Crochet the Beak and Wattle:

Beak

with gold

ch 4, starting in the 2nd ch from hook dc3tog

Finish off, cut yarn leaving long end for sewing

Wattle

with red

ch 5, hdc in 2nd ch from hook, sc in next ch, slip stitch in last 2

Finish off, cut yarn leaving end for sewing

Sew the beak and wattle to the head just below eyes

STEP SIX

Make 2- with gold yarn

*You will make 3 "toes" first and then start crocheting in the round as you make the legs

Thanksgiving Crochet

Row 1: [ch3, dc in first ch, ch 1, slip stitch in first ch] repeat 2 more times (3 dc "toes")

Row 2: ch 1, turn, sc in the top of each toe, ch 3

*this row you will begin working in the round by working in the sc across the front and the ch across the back

Row 3: 1 sc in each of the 3 sc across front of foot, 3 sc in ch (6 sc)

Row 4-9: 1 sc in each stitch (6 sc)

Finish off, cut yarn leaving ends for sewing

Sew the legs to the bottom front of the body

STEP SEVEN

Crochet the Feathers:

Make 5- 1 each blue, orange, red, green, gold

Thanksgiving Crochet

begin with a magic ring (mr)

Round 1: in mr, ch 1, 4 sc (4 sc)

Round 2: [2 sc in first stitch, 1 sc in next] repeat (6 sc)

Round 3: [2 sc in first stitch, 1 sc in next 2] repeat (8 sc)

Round 4: [2 sc in first stitch, 1 sc in next 3] repeat (10 sc)

Round 5: [2 sc in first stitch, 1 sc in next 4] repeat (12 sc)

Round 6-8: 1 sc in each stitch (12 sc)

Round 9: [2 sc in first stitch, 1 sc in next 5] repeat (14 sc)

Round 10-14: 1 sc in each stitch (14 sc)

Round 15: [sc2tog, sc in next 5] repeat (12 sc)

Round 16: 1 sc in each stitch (12 sc)

Round 17: [sc2tog, sc in next 4] (10 sc)

Finish off, cut yarn leaving long end for sewing

Sew feathers to back of turkey in a semicircle shape

Tiny Little Turkey

Supplies:

G – hook

Medium weight (4) yarn: brown, yellow, and any color of choice for feathers

Thanksgiving Crochet

Safety eyes (used 9mm) or black embroidery floss for eyes

Poly-fil stuffing

Yarn needle

_**Terms:**

ch – chain

sc – single crochet

inc – increase (2 single crochets in same hook)

dec – decrease (crochet 2 stitches together)

slp st – slip stitch

**Head/Body:**

Using brown, ch 2

1. sc 5 in second ch from hook – 5

2. 2sc in each st around – 10

3. (sc, inc)5x – 15

4. (sc 2, inc)5x – 20

5-8. sc around – 20

9. (sc 2, dec)5x – 15

10. sc around – 15

If using safety eyes, attach to the sides of the head now. I put mine in between row #4&5

Begin stuffing

11. (sc, dec)5x – 10

12-13. sc around – 10

14. (sc, inc)3x, sc 4 – 13

15. (sc 2, inc)3x, sc 4 – 16

16. (sc 2, inc)4x – 20

17. (sc 3, inc)5x – 25

18-21. sc around – 25

22. (sc 3, dec)5x – 20

23. (sc 2, dec)5x – 15

24. (sc, dec)5x – 10

25. dec 6, sew shut, fasten off, weave in ends

Beak:

Using yellow, Ch 2

1. 4sc in the second ch from hook – 4

2. 2sc in each st around – 8

3. sc around – 8

4. (sc, inc)4x – 12

5. sc around – 12

Fasten off, leave long tail for sewing.

Wings: Make two

Using brown, ch 2

1. 5sc in second ch from hook – 5

2. 2sc in each st around – 10

3-7. sc around – 10 each row

8. dec 4 – 6

9-11. sc around – 6 each row

Whip st closed (do not stuff) leave long tail for sewing.

Legs: Make two

Using yellow, ch 2

1. 6sc in the second ch from hk – 6

2. 2sc in each st around – 12

3. (sc, inc)6x – 18

4-5. sc around – 18 each row

6. (sc, dec)6x – 12

7. dec 3, sc 5 – 9

8. sc, dec 2, sc 4 – 7

Begin stuffing.

9-12. sc around – 7 each row

Do not stuff last two rows of leg. Sew shut flat. Leave long tail for

Thanksgiving Crochet

sewing to body

**Feathers**: **make at least four of each**

Using brown ch 13

1.starting in second ch from hk, sc 10, slp st 2 – 12

2. ch 1, turn, slp st 3, sc 8, inc – 13

3. Now continuing around the back of the chain: inc, sc 8, slp st 3 – 13

From this point, you will have 26 stitches around with a flat base.

4. ch 1, turn, slp st 5, sc 7, inc, sc, inc, sc 7, slp st 5- 29

Fasten off, leave long tail for sewing.

Using any color you choose and an F-hook

Follow the pattern for the feather base row 1-3.

Leave a long tail, sew onto the brown base

Wattle: Make two

Using red

Ch 4

Thanksgiving Crochet

1. starting in second ch from hk, slp st 2.

Fasten off, leave long tail for sewing.

Assembly:

Sew the beak on stuffing lightly as you go.

Sew wattles under the beak.

Sew on the feathers.

Sew on wings.

Sew on legs

Finished size: 4 1/2 inches sitting down.

Made in United States
Orlando, FL
28 September 2024

52054315R00036